Pathways
to Relationship

Series Preface

The volumes in NCP's "7 x 4" series offer a meditation a day for four weeks, a bite of food for thought, a reflection that lets a reader ponder the spiritual significance of each and every day. Small enough to slip into a purse or coat pocket, these books fit easily into everyday routines.

Pathways to Relationship

Four Weeks on Simplicity, Gentleness,
Humility, Friendship

Robert F. Morneau

New City Press
Hyde Park, New York

Published in the United States by New City Press
202 Cardinal Rd., Hyde Park, NY 12538
www.newcitypress.com

Cover design by Durva Correia

Library of Congress Cataloging-in-Publication Data:

Morneau, Robert F., 1938-
    Pathways to relationship : four weeks on simplicity, gentleness, humility,
friendship / Robert F. Morneau.
        p. cm. — (7 x 4: a meditation a day for four weeks)
    ISBN 978-1-56548-317-0 (pbk. : alk. paper) 1. Interpersonal relations—
Religious aspects—Christianity—Meditations.
I. Title.
 BV4597.52.M66 2009
 242'.2—dc22   2008053421

Printed in the United States of America

Contents

one
Simplicity

two
Gentleness

three
Humility

four
Friendship

Foreword

Just as the theological virtues of faith, hope, and charity nurture our relationships with God, and just as the moral virtues of prudence, justice, fortitude, and temperance foster a strong and vibrant moral life, so too the social virtues aid us in relating well with others in our daily life. In her personal journal, Raissa Maritain, wife of the noted French philosopher Jacques Maritain, wrote:

> Yesterday I had a good morning. Once again when I recollect myself, I again find the same simple demands of God: gentleness, humility, charity, interior simplicity; nothing else is asked of me. And suddenly I saw clearly why these virtues are demanded, because through them the soul becomes habitable for God and for one's neighbor in an intimate and permanent way. They make a pleasant cell of it. Hardness and pride repel, complexity disquiets. But humility and gentleness welcome, simplicity reassures. These "passive" virtues have an eminently social character.
>
> *(Raissa Maritain)*

This book is an invitation to "recollect" one-self, to pause as we journey through life to reflect upon our relationships and the virtues that promote character and quality of life. What we attend to is a good indicator of who we are and what we value. By attending to the virtues, be they theological, moral, or social, we strive to reach our full potential and to serve both the common good and the Kingdom of God.

Of Raissa Maritain's four demands, this small volume will address three: simplicity, gentleness, and humility. Since I touched on charity in a previous volume, I have selected a variety of other virtues — respect, graciousness, friendship, wit, forgiveness, and others — to round out the fourth week. In a culture of much incivility, a return to basic virtues might help create an atmosphere of love, light, and life.

I sense that Raissa Maritain might assure us of this: "Tomorrow will bring a good morning if today we strive to live virtuously!"

Simplicity

one

Willing One Thing

Advances in science have demonstrated, beyond a doubt, the complexity of life. It is undeniably complicated and convoluted. Yet, it is possible to find a center, a unity that orders life's diverse dimensions be they physical or psychological, social or political, religious or cultural. We live with the hope that peace is possible. By willing one thing, by willing God's will, we can achieve some tranquility on the turbulent seas of life.

> Now I see that I was all mixed up, that I had fragmented my life into many sections that did not really form a unity. The question is not, "Do I have time to prepare?" but, "Do I live in a state of preparedness?" When God is my only concern, when God is the center of my interest, when all my prayers, reading, my studying, my speaking, and writing serve only to know God better and to make him known better, then there is no basis for anxiety or stage fright. Then I can live in such a state of preparedness and trust that speaking

from the heart is also speaking to the heart. My fears and my resulting fatigue over the last three years might well be diagnosed as a lack of single-mindedness, as a lack of one-eyedness, as a lack of simplicity. Indeed, how divided my heart has been and still is! I want to love God, but also to make a career. I want to be a good Christian, but also have my successes as a teacher, preacher, or speaker. I want to be close to Christ, but also popular and liked by many people. No wonder that living becomes a tiring enterprise. The characteristic of a saint is, to borrow Kierkegaard's words, "To will one thing." Well, I will more than one thing, am double-hearted, double-minded, and have a very divided loyalty.

(Henri J. M. Nouwen)

Question: What is your description or definition of a saint? Does that description involve the virtue of simplicity?

Prayer: Lord Jesus, you told Martha that only one thing is necessary in life. That one thing is to know and do your Father's will. Help us to understand the divine plan. May we, like the prophet Micah tells us, "act justly, love tenderly, walk humbly with you" (see Micah 6:8). Nothing more is asked.

2 Simplify! Simplify!

Whoever coined the phrase — "The more the merrier" — did not have a good grasp of psychology. There is just so much … and so many … that the human spirit can handle. A vital part of self-knowledge is to know how much weight one can bear and how many balls one can juggle. In our age of activity and multi-tasking, it is necessary to learn to "downsize" activities and relationships to a proportion that protects healthy living. Thoreau's 19th-century cry echoes down the ages.

> *Simplicity, simplicity, simplicity! I say, let your affairs be as two or three, and not a hundred or a thousand; instead of a million count half a dozen, and keep your account on your thumb-nail. In the midst of this chopping sea of civilized life, such are the clouds and storms and quicksands and thousand-and-one items to be allowed for, that a man has to live, if he would not founder and go to the bottom and not make his port at all, by dead reckoning, and he must be a great calculator indeed who succeeds. Simplify, simplify. Instead of three*

meals a day, if it be necessary eat but one; instead of a hundred dishes, five; and reduce other things in proportion.

(Henry David Thoreau)

Question: What can you do to simplify your life? Is this simplifying more interior or exterior?

Prayer: Lord Jesus, you had many affairs to attend to: the formation of the disciples, the preaching of the Kingdom, the healing of the sick. Amid all these events and activities, you centered everything on your relationship with the Father. Help us do the same.

3 Our Vast Universe

The Hubble telescope has unveiled the incredible vastness of the universe. Our finite imagination staggers before such immensity. Just as oceans and mountains astounded pioneers at first view, so now galaxy upon galaxy, numbering in the billions, confront us. Not surprisingly, a knowledgeable scientist like Loren Eiseley concludes that simplicity has no part in his belief system. Yet the human heart desires the satellites of simplicity, harmony and unity, and the great ones among us have experienced this grace. Doubting does not negate the possibility or the reality.

"Well," I added, as the duck paddled along slowly, displaying its intricately patterned feathers, "that's just the way I feel right now, as though the universe were too frighteningly queer to be understood by minds like ours. It's not a popular view. One is suppose to flourish Occam's razor and reduce hypotheses about a complex world to human proportions. Certainly I try. Mostly I come out feeling that whatever else the universe may be, its

so-called simplicity is a trick, perhaps like that bird out there. I know we have learned a lot, but the scope is too vast for us. Every now and then if we look behind us, everything has changed. It isn't precisely that nature tricks us. We trick ourselves with our own ingenuity. I don't believe in simplicity.

(Loren Eiseley)

Question: What thoughts run through your mind when you stand under the starry, starry sky? In what or in whom do you ground the possibility of simplicity?

Prayer: Lord Jesus, our finite minds and hearts are overwhelmed by the immensity of truth and nature. Give us your wisdom to understand the essence of things. Remove our doubt and confusion and fill us with the beauty of your Presence.

4 The Simplicity of Simplicity

Is it possible that in life only one thing really matters: holy obedience? If we are responsive to God — the true Shepherd, the divine Center, the heavenly Monitor — then our relationships and activities will be properly ordered. Disobedience destroys simplicity. When we do it our way and go off on our own, complexity settles in around our hearts. Then, our souls know no peace.

The joyful paradox in all this is that while simplicity is complex it is also simple. In the final analysis we are not the ones who have to untangle all the intricacies of our complex world. There are not many things we have to keep in mind — in fact, only one: to be attentive to the voice of the true Shepherd. There are not many decisions we have to make — in fact, only one: to seek first his Kingdom and righteousness. There are not many tasks we have to do — in fact, only one: to obey him in all things. As Soren Kierkegaard understood so clearly, we are honed down to only one thing, and that is the simplicity of sim-

plicity. This is why the inward reality of holy obedience to the divine Center is so central to everything about simplicity. Without that we will become frustrated and stymied by the complexity of it all. With it life is ordered and filled with peace. The only thing we have to do is be, at every moment, attentive to the heavenly Monitor. And as we are, there comes welling up whispers of Divine guidance and love that make life radiant.

(Richard J. Foster)

Question: In what sense is obedience the core of simplicity? Have you experienced the cause/effect relationship of disobedience and complexity?

Prayer: Lord Jesus, give us obedient, discerning hearts. Too often we venture off on our own, seeking our own plans and strange designs. Attune our ears to the sound of your gracious voice; mold our hearts into havens for the Holy Spirit.

Simplicity and Commitment

To have but one commitment would appear to bring about an authentic simplicity. Letting one purpose or goal dominate life would seem to eradicate the question of complexity. Yet at various levels and to various degrees we all have a series of commitments, be they religious, social, political, or moral. Commitment, worthy and esteemed as it is, must be framed in the context of our full humanity.

> Commitment is bound to be painful, for its reverse side, so to speak, is renunciation. Each one has to establish a hierarchy of commitments, and concentrate his energies on those that stand at the top of the scale. There may even be one, an "ultimate concern" in Tillich's phrase, which governs all the others. It is where commitment is limited that we see most strikingly its contribution to the establishment of a definite character and identity. Hauer has remarked that "the clearest example of character is one in which a life is dominated by one all-consuming purpose or direction." I think myself however that

where one commitment, however admirable, is exalted to this almost terrifying level, the danger of fanaticism is great, and that a more balanced humanity requires a few back commitments (I shall try later to say what these might be). Even a commitment to God cannot (and should not) abolish my commitment to my family or to society, as we saw in our discussion of Kierkegaard's treatment of the Abraham story. I think too that, important though commitment and conscience are in the quest for humanity, there is a danger of becoming too moralistic and puritanical if one exaggerates the agonies of resolve and renunciation and forgets that a fully human existence also has its time of relaxation, play, and humor. We do not have to insist on a reason for everything, and later we shall ask about the role of play, humor and art in life.

(John Macquarrie)

Question: What is the master commitment in your life right now? How do other commitments relate to that dominant one?

Prayer: Lord Jesus, you were committed to the Father's will. In that you found simplicity of purpose. Teach us how to connect all of our commitments to that single one and thereby live in joyful simplicity.

6 Simplicity and Challenges

Like it or not, we all have many irons in the fire. Given that we are social creatures with physical, intellectual, cultural, and political concerns, we have to address all these dimensions. These numerous challenges seem to preclude the possibility of simplicity. Again we are drawn back to that basic struggle between life and death, love and hate, grace and sin. Simplicity here means that, whatever our circumstances, we seek to discern the loving and compassionate response. In this mode of living, with God's help, simplicity becomes possible.

> *They [students] know the age-old struggle between grace and sin. Their challenges sound familiar: forming their personal identity, developing good friendships, finding a life partner, choosing a career, appropriating their religious heritage, cultivating habits of good citizenship, and deciding how to relate to the dominant culture.*
>
> *(James J. Bacik and Kevin E. Anderson)*

Question: Of the challenges listed above, which have you already negotiated? How are you dealing with the ones remaining?

Prayer: Jesus, you had to relate to the political and cultural forces of your day. You had to balance your relationships with the disciples and other groups. Teach us the art of living with a simple heart; help us to follow in your way.

Center and Circumference

Recent years have seen much emphasis on "centering prayer." It invites individuals and communities to seek inner stillness and focus attention on God. Once this prayer "kicks in," daily life takes on a graced simplicity and unity. Now all is referred to God as the center of life; even though some days are chaotic, the circumference and center come into unison.

We know how an absorbing devotion to a great ideal or, more profoundly still, to a beloved person, simplifies and unifies life. And to the soul that is wholly bent upon God, the thousand fretting cares and vexing problems that tear the lives of others to pieces simply cease to exist. With the submerging of the irrelevant, the soul is free to give itself to that which really matters. Life becomes henceforth triumphantly effective. It is no more the happy hunting-ground of vagrant impulses and futile efforts; it is the theater of divine activity, the

sphere of creative power. Its circumference is governed from the center.

(Brigid E. Herman)

Question: How does devotion to an ideal simplify and unify your life? How do you obtain or receive that devotion?

Prayer: Lord Jesus, you are the Center of our lives. May everything that we say and do find its reference point in you. May everything that you desire reach out to the circumference of our lives and enliven us with your grace.

Gentleness

two

A Diligent Gentleness

Too easily do we become hard of heart. In our striving for perfection and success, we tend to become self-reliant and fail to implore the assistance of God. In the end, our efforts are minimal unless imbued with a spirit of love and gentleness. Beyond doubt, we are to work hard in doing what God asks of us, but the manner in which we perform that service is crucial. We are to live our days with a gentle and humble heart. Only with God's help can we accomplish this.

Don't lose any opportunity, however small, of being gentle toward everyone. Don't rely on your own efforts to succeed in your various undertakings, but only on God's help. Then rest in His care of you, confident that He will do what is best for you, provided that you, for your part, work diligently and gently. I say "gently" because a tense diligence is harmful both to our heart and to our task and is not really diligence, but over-eagerness and anxiety.

(Francis de Sales, Jane de Chantal)

Question: How gentle are you toward others and yourself? Are diligence and gentleness truly compatible?

Prayer: Lord Jesus, you who are gentle and humble of heart, help us to emulate you in our dealings with others and ourselves. May we strive diligently to follow in your way, but always with a gentle and compassionate heart. Send us your Spirit of gentleness.

2 Inborn Gentleness

Mohandas K. Gandhi truly witnessed to a life of dialogue and civility. More, he strove to nurture an inner attitude of gentleness that colored all his words and deeds. Struggling against great odds and opposed on many sides, he refrained from harshness and incivility. By some grace he was able to witness to a way of life that respected all, even those individuals who were cruel and oppressive.

> Experience has taught me that civility is the most difficult part of Satyagrahi. Civility does not here mean the mere outward gentleness of speech cultivated for the occasion, but an inborn gentleness and desire to do the opponent good. These should show themselves in every act of a Satyagrahi.

(Mohandas K. Gandhi)

Question: What do you understand by an "in-born gentleness"? In what ways do civility and gentleness differ?

Prayer: Lord Jesus, you instruct us to love our enemies. We need your Spirit if we are to be gentle and loving to those who oppose us. May what we say and do flow out of a truly gentle heart.

A Rude Gentleness

Does divinity need rudeness to achieve its goal of transforming humanity into divinity? Perhaps we are once again in the land of semantics. St. Paul tells us that love is never rude. Since God is love, how can the Almighty be rude? Maybe the answer lies in the surgeon's knife: the doctor must hurt in order to heal, and does so out of love and compassion. In the end, God's gentleness finds ironic expressions.

God Is Not Nice

God is not nice.
Frankly I would think twice
before inviting him to tea.
He would bore us with long silences
and sit and crumble cake
and eye us owlishly.

I am sure I would be hard pressed
before I would make a house guest
of this king. He would untidy
my chaste rooms with sudden

gusts of grandeur, and I would be picking up
all day after the Almighty.

In truth I would become delirious
living with this imperious Lover.
He would rip the fine design
I have stitched for my pleasant days,
saying, "I must be rude
if I am to be divine."

(Edward Seifert)

Question: Can rudeness ever be justified? Is there such a thing as rude gentleness?

Prayer: Lord Jesus, in the temple you drove out the money changers. In talking with the elders of the people, you called them vipers and hypocrites. Yet, you are our gentle Lord who is not afraid to express love in strong language.

4 Traits of a Gentleman

It is good to be advised by the wise. As they pass on the valuable lessons from life, we grow in moral and spiritual stature. Some advice is imperative: speak kindly, love tenderly, work diligently. Other advice is prohibitive specifying what "not" to do: don't gossip, don't correct people in public, don't take what is not yours. Our education does not end in kindergarten: let us be attuned to wisdom from whatever source.

She began by explaining to me that a gentleman, or, as she would say, "a man of breeding," is known not so much by what he does as by what he will not do. First and foremost, he never imputes a base motive to anyone else. If someone is rude to him, he assumes that the rudeness is unintentional. If he knows that it is intentional, he acts as if it were not. He never insulted anyone himself except by intention. He never met anger with anger. He never patronized anyone because he never assumed that he knew more than anyone else or that uneducated people are unintelli-

gent. He never corrected (or smiled at) other people's slips. "Always," my mother would say, "allow other people the luxury of being mistaken. They will find out for themselves soon enough. If they don't, they are the kind of people in whom it does not matter."

(Whittaker Chambers)

Question: Which qualities of a gentle person do you identify with? What positive characteristics of a gentle person would you add to those mentioned in this passage?

Prayer: Lord Jesus, as you respected and reverenced everyone you met, help us to do the same. Every person has dignity and deserves our kindness. Remove all rudeness from our hearts.

5 The Influence of Gentleness

There is a mystery about gentleness. Why does it exert such a power over the human heart? And when that virtue dwells in a saintly soul like St. Francis of Assisi, hundreds of thousands of people are fascinated and astonished. Perhaps gentleness says to us that we can relax and feel safe and important. Perhaps gentleness affirms our very being and convinces us that we can delight in existence. Perhaps gentleness is sheer beauty, sheer grace.

> But the woman in turn subjugates the man by the mystery of gentleness in beauty, and the saint has always charmed the world by something similar. Mankind is susceptible and suggestible in opposite directions, and the rivalry of influences is unsleeping. The saintly and the worldly ideal pursue their feud in literature as much as in real life.
>
> (William James)

Question: How much does gentleness influence your life? How have you influenced others by your gentleness?

Prayer: Lord Jesus, the influence of your gentle grace is indeed unsleeping. Your love charms us and makes us whole. Your gentle care heals us and makes us joyful. Make us agents and instruments of your gentle Spirit.

6 This Ferocious Age

The volume of violence in the last hundred years defies adequate description. Nations and individuals alike have pursued ferocious policies. Wars and terrorism have become a way of life. It is not surprising then that such an era ignores the virtues of gentleness and courtesy. It prefers to destroy those it considers an enemy rather than offer them an affable smile. Delicate souls will find this a difficult time, but they must be true to themselves and refuse to return violence for violence.

> Courtesy, harmony, balance, happiness, life's sweetness — all these were virtues and joys which we had to be brave enough to bid adieu; they belonged to other ages, past or future. Every age has its own countenance. The countenance of our age was ferocious, and delicate souls dared not look it straight in the eye.
>
> (Nikos Kazantzakis)

Question: In our ferocious age is gentleness possible or even advisable?

Prayer: Lord Jesus, your peace is opposed to ferocity and violence. Whatever the countenance of our age, may we not respond with an eye for an eye. Rather, like you, may we always be courteous and gentle, regardless of the circumstances.

7 Gentleness: A Fruit of the Spirit

The great St. Paul knew much about the life of virtue. Often he wrote about the great theological virtues — faith, hope, and charity — leading to knowledge of and union with God. The moral virtues — prudence, justice, fortitude, and temperance — were also great concerns of this apostle to the Gentiles. He also discoursed on the social virtues — humility, simplicity, and gentleness. To the Galatians, Paul described the fruits of the flesh and the fruits of the Holy Spirit. These two ways of life lie before all of us and we must choose.

Now the works of the flesh are obvious: fornication, impurity, licentiousness, idolatry, sorcery, enmities, strife, jealousy, anger, quarrels, dissensions, factions, envy, drunkenness, carousing, and things like these. I am warning you, as I have warned you before: those who do such things will not inherit the kingdom of God. By contrast, the fruit of the Spirit is love, joy, peace, patience, kindness, generos-

ity, faithfulness, gentleness, and self-control. There is no law against such things.

(Galatians 5:19–23)

Questions: What is the relationship between gentleness and the other fruits of the Holy Spirit?

Prayer: Lord Jesus, send your Spirit into our hearts. Drive out all evil and darkness; fill us with your light and love. Make us truly gentle and humble of heart.

Humility

three

Humility: Nothing but Truth

St. Francis of Assisi is universally acclaimed because he was a man of truth. He knew who he was; he had no pretense. He saw everything he had and every talent he possessed as a gift from God. Those who let humility dominate the heart experience two things: freedom and joy. The humble person is neither enslaved by the lie nor saddened over the possibility of being "discovered." Humility's birth father is Truth.

We all tend to be infatuated with the idea of strength — that is why definitions of prayer in terms of "force" appeal to us so strongly — but we fail to realize that all true strength is grounded in humility. We still relegate humility to the pale ranks of passive virtues and ornamental graces, whereas in its legitimate development it is a stout and soldierly quality. Indeed, humility is simply a sense of reality and proportion. It is grounded upon knowledge of the truth about ourselves and about God. "The reason God is so great a lover of

humility," says St. Vincent de Paul, with his characteristic forthrightness, "is that he is a great lover of truth. Now humility is nothing but truth, while pride is nothing but lying."

(Brigid E. Herman)

Question: How do you maintain a sense of reality and proportion? In what sense is pride nothing but a lie?

Prayer: Lord Jesus, open our minds to the truth of things. Pour forth the light of your Spirit that we may live in the reality of things and avoid the darkness of the lie.

2 Humility: Key to Faith; Perfection of Joy

We tend to either overestimate or underestimate people, places, and things. And when we do, we feel some degree of disappointment, even frustration. What value do we assign to a career, a relationship, a piece of property or bank account? To "get it right" puts things in perspective and keeps us in the land of reality. Humility calls for graced estimation.

It is almost impossible to overestimate the value of true humility and its power in the spiritual life. For the beginning of humility is the beginning of blessedness and the consummation of humility is the perfection of joy. Humility contains in itself the answer to all the great problems of the life of the soul. It is the only key to faith, with which the spiritual life begins: for faith and humility are inseparable. In perfect humility all selfishness disappears and your soul no longer lives for itself or in it-

self but for God: and it is lost and submerged in Him and transformed into Him.

(Thomas Merton)

Question: What value do you assign to humility, to faith, and to joy? In what ways are these values interconnected?

Prayer: Lord Jesus, we beg for the gift and grace of humility. Help us to forget ourselves so that we may live in you and do the Father's will. Without this grace, we are bound to fail.

Humility:
The Act of
Acceptance

Humility is not optional. Rather, it is fundamental to our spiritual and social life. When pride holds sway, we live in falsity and enslavement. When we embrace humility, we are free and dwell in the truth. A radical self-acceptance that neither exaggerates our talents nor minimizes our graces is essential. Refusing to accept who we are means being troubled guests on this long, human journey.

Humility is truth, accepting the real facts about ourselves, and sometimes we sin against it by overconfidence, by exaggerating our gifts and putting all our trust in strength which is largely illusory; but sometimes we sin in the opposite sense, by minimizing our gifts, by pretending we are less or worse than we really are. Truth lies in accepting ourselves while realizing both that whatever good there is in us comes from God and that, however insignificant our endowments are, God is quite capable of

achieving through us the ends He desires if only we accept His will and trust in Him.

(Gerald Vann, O. P., and
P. K. Meagher, O. P.)

Question: Why is self-acceptance so difficult? And a further question: is self-acceptance possible without deep self-knowledge?

Prayer: Lord Jesus, you accepted the people who came into your life, whatever their circumstances. We believe that you accept us. Give us the grace to accept ourselves and to walk the path of humility.

4 Humility and Humiliation

It is difficult to see how humiliation can become a creative force. When we blush with shame we want to run and hide. Yet in the darkness of humiliation, we can find much grace as we are led, once again, down the path of humility. Our journey is filled with many temptations toward pride and arrogance. Humiliations tend to counter these egoistical forces and keep us on the narrow path of humility.

> Years ago, someone told me that humility is central to the spiritual life. That made sense to me: I was proud to think of myself as humble! But this person did not tell me that the path to humility, for some of us at least, goes through humiliation, where we are brought low, rendered powerless, stripped of pretenses and defenses, and left feeling fraudulent, empty, and useless — a humiliation that allows us to regrow our lives from the ground up, from the humus of common ground.
>
> (Parker Palmer)

The spiritual journey is not a success story, but a series of diminutions of self. Saint Bernard of Clairvaux, the 12th century Cistercian Abbot, taught that humiliation is the path to humility. In those who have a low self-image, there may be some confusion between humility and the neurotic tendency to put oneself down. The latter, of course, is not humility. The language of humility can be misunderstood. Basically, it is the experiential awareness, born of the divine light, that without God's protection we are capable of every sin. The night of the spirit is an intensive course in humility.

(Thomas Keating)

Question: What is the difference between humility and humiliation in your experience? Do the two often occur together?

Prayer: Lord Jesus, in times of humiliation, you turned to your Father in radical trust. Help us who follow in your way. May every humiliation deepen our humility.

5 A Hiding Place

There is an intimate connection between God's will and the virtue of humility. The person who embraces all the weathers of the divine design has the possibility of being truly humble and, dare we say, happy. In that deep and grateful embrace of all the circumstances of one's life humility is born. It demands courage as well as stillness, a silence that contemplates the stirrings of grace. In the end it comes down to the experiential knowledge that one is loved and that God can be trusted.

Humility

Humility is to be still
under the weathers of God's will.

It is to have no hurt surprise
when morning's ruddy promise dies,

when the wind and drought destroy, or sweet
spring rains apostatize in sleet,

or when the mind and month remark
a superfluity of dark.

It is to have no troubled care
for human weathers anywhere.

And yet it is to take the good
with the warm hands of gratitude.

Humility is to have a place
deep in the secret of God's face

where one can know, past all surmise,
that God's great will alone is wise,

where one is loved, where one can trust
a strength not circumscribed by dust.

It is to have a place to hide
when all is hurricane outside.

(Jessica Powers)

Question: Where do you go when the hurricanes of life arise? Does humility offer a special place?

Prayer: Lord Jesus, help us to discern your Father's will and to embrace it with humility and joy. Send your Spirit to govern our days, stormy or not.

6
Humility = Self-Knowledge

In Christian tradition, pride is one of the capital sins (the others: greed, anger, sloth, gluttony, envy, and lust). Sin implies both knowledge and freedom. Yet, there is something simply stupid about pride and arrogance. The sin of pride fails to recognize our status as creatures. Everything we have and are comes from God. To claim that what we are or do is ultimately of our own making simply doesn't make sense. One suspects that other creatures, such as ants and bumblebees, know this quite clearly.

> *Pride is far more stupidity than a sin. It is an inability to grasp the facts, to realize our small creaturely status and helplessness. It is the failure to see that our most magnificent achievements are no more than the success of an ant handling a rather larger bit of straw than that manipulated by another ant. This is why spiritual specialists insist that humility is the same thing as self-knowledge.*
>
> *(Evelyn Underhill)*

Question: What makes pride ultimately rather humorous? Nevertheless, why are pride and arrogance ultimately so sad?

Prayer: Lord Jesus, we stand in need of your help at every moment. Left to ourselves, we can do nothing of ultimate importance. Bless us, your disciples, with insight and humility.

7 Christian Humility

As much as we would delight in comprehending the mystery of God's kingdom, we are given only a glimpse. Yet, that "joy" of what is to come should be sufficient to do two things: keep us humble and keep us longing for the fullness of God's sway in our lives. Probably nothing is more devastating to the spiritual life than the sin of presumption. If it is not the sin against the Holy Spirit, it comes very close.

> How does the Gospel of Jesus compare with Brahmanism and Buddhism? When meeting them, it becomes first of all conscious of its own simplicity. Brahmanism and Buddhism believe that they have lifted the curtain and found the solution to the riddles of the world and of human life. This arrogance of those who "know," we find in Indian literature. Those who work in India find it in the men with whom they have to deal. It is an important feature of the character of the Indian religion. Jesus does not lead us into such presumption, but into humility. He wakens in us a longing to get a glimpse of the mystery

of the Kingdom of God. In I Cor. xiii the apostle Paul uses powerful words to express the thought that at best "we know in part."

(Albert Schweitzer)

Question: In your experience is the dominant characteristic of Christianity humility or arrogance?

Prayer: Lord Jesus, you continue to teach us about the mystery of your Father's kingdom. Grant us the humility to approach on soft feet the mystery of God's reign. Only your wisdom will keep us from presumption.

Friendship

four

The Art of Making Room

Receiving hospitality from others is one of life's great graces. When we open our minds and hearts to others with sincerity and generosity, joy and peace await us. Too often doors and hearts are closed. People remain out in the cold. Interestingly, the more we open our hearts to hospitality, the more room we have for ourselves. We emulate our God in a supreme way by being hospitable.

The celebrating community can bring itself alive when all the members of the community acknowledge a direct and primary responsibility of hospitality to one another. Hospitality best translates the meaning of Christian community love. Hospitality is a form of caring enough for others to give them space in your life and to welcome them in. Hospitality says: "There is room right now for you in my life and I want to make it clear to you right now that there is room, and I am hoping that there is room now in your life for me." Hospitality is precise and careful in its demands. It does

not seek any long-term friendship or lasting relationships. It asks for presence and attention from each member of the community for the duration of the celebration.

(Eugene A. Walsh, S.S.)

Question: How do you make room for others in your life? How present and attentive are you to others?

Prayer: Lord Jesus, you welcomed others into your life with loving attentiveness. Teach us the art of hospitality. May we make room in our hearts for all we meet, especially the lost and lonely.

A Distant Friendship

Holding another in regard, indeed with attention, is the core of respect. Like Red Skelton's character Freddie the Freeloader, who believed that everyone was made to the image and likeness of God, seeing the dignity of each person that leads to assigning a sense of worth to every individual. This dignity rests not upon some unique charism or major accomplishment but upon simply being there, bearing the gift of existence. Respect, a "distant friendship," creates a society of rich civility.

> Yet what love is in its own, narrowly circumscribed sphere, respect is in the larger domain of human affairs. Respect, not unlike the Aristotelian philia politike, is a kind of "friendship" without intimacy and without closeness; it is a regard for the person from the distance which the space of the world puts between us, and this regard is independent of qualities which we may admire or of achievements which we may highly esteem.
>
> (Hannah Arendt)

Question: How does respect differ from intimacy? What is the relationship between respect and friendship?

Prayer: Lord Jesus, may your grace help us to see — *respicere* — every person we meet and see in them the image of God. Remove the blindness that prevents us from truly seeing the basic goodness in every person.

Gracious Because Graced

In one of his essays, Ralph Waldo Emerson commented: "I saw a gracious gentleman who adapts his conversation to the form of the head of the man he talks with!" Here is the essence of graciousness, an absence of condescension or any form of arrogance. When present, this virtue creates an atmosphere both pleasant and affable. When absent, tension and considerable discomfort reign. Graced People, those who know that they are loved, are empowered to be gracious.

It was the way one treated guests, a friendly, pleasant manner, without letting them see one's own moods or discontent; making conversation in spite of one's disinclination or the unresponsiveness of the other person; showing interest, not just making a pretense of it, even when one's own inclination at the moment led elsewhere.

(Hans Urs von Balthasar)

Question: Who in your life exemplified graciousness? What characteristics did they demonstrate?

Prayer: Lord Jesus, you are generous and gracious. Send forth your Spirit of graciousness into our hearts and homes. Make them pleasant and friendly. Make them an abode of peace.

4 The Virtue of Friendship

Friendship implies the great social virtue of affability, that beautiful friendliness that opens minds and hearts to one another. By contrast, aloofness and cool reserve close the door to the warmth and affection of intimacy. In the animal world, black labs are affable, capable of great friendship. German shepherds, on the other hand, are fearsome and under the command of one master. For us humans, however, virtue is more than temperament. Virtue lived makes peace and joy possible. And are peace and joy possible without the virtue of friendship, graced affability?

> Then, when all is done, a person of related mind, a brother or sister by nature, comes to us so softly and easily, so nearly and intimately, as if it were the blood in our proper veins, that we feel as if someone was gone, instead of another having come; we are utterly relieved and refreshed; it is a sort of joyful solitude.
>
> (Ralph Waldo Emerson)

Life goes headlong. We chase some flying scheme, or we are hunted by some fear or command behind us. But if suddenly we encounter a friend, we pause; our heat and hurry look foolish enough; now pause, now possession is required, and the power to swell the moment from the resources of the heart. The moment is all, in all noble relations.

(Ralph Waldo Emerson)

Question: What role has the virtue of friendship played in your life? To whom have you offered the gift of friendship?

Prayer: Lord Jesus, you did not call your disciples servants, but friends. May we embrace that gift and treasure, this love and affection you have for us.

The Virtue of Humor

Humor plays a major role in social relationships. Laughter, as well as variety, is the spice of life. The ability to see the incongruity of things, to have a sense of proportion, to be cheerful in a very serious world, all indicate mental health. Humorlessness is deadly. A lack of frivolity is a sad commentary on life. Wit and humor oil our relationships and help to save us from the universal disease of narcissism.

> He [Roncalli — Pope John XXIII] practiced a sort of intuitive diplomacy. He had a sure sense of when it was safe to ignore protocol and when silence was his strongest ally. His wit was based on intelligence, restraint, and sensitivity — as genuine wit always is. But in the end he was popular and hence, successful, because beneath the light touch lay the deepest of feelings about men and issues.
>
> (Lawrence Elliott)

Question: What role does humor play in your social and spiritual life? How does wit differ from ridicule or sarcasm?

Prayer: Lord Jesus, guide us in the way of truth and humor. Give us both the grace to be both serious and lighthearted, to be responsible and to have fun. Help us to see the humor in your eyes and your delight in our frail humanity.

6 The Machinery of Forgiveness

In social life, it is easy to fall into offensive behavior. Be it a word or deed, an attitude or disposition, we can hurt one another in many ways. Thus, we have great need for forgiveness. Peace comes only if we acknowledge the separation and alienation produced by negative behavior. Peace is possible only through the art of forgiveness. A family, community, or society without the machinery or apparatus of forgiveness is to be pitied.

> *Hannah Arendt had discerned that this [mercy/forgiveness] was Jesus' most endangering action because if a society does not have an apparatus for forgiveness then its members are fated to live forever with the consequences of any violation. Thus the refusal to forgive sin (or the management of the machinery of forgiveness) amounts to enormous social control.*
>
> *(Walter Brueggemann)*

Forgiveness is the answer to the child's dream of a miracle by which what is broken is made whole again, what is soiled is again made clean. The dream explains why we need to be forgiven, and why we must forgive. In the presence of God, nothing stands between Him and us — we are forgiven. But we cannot feel His presence if anything is allowed to stand between ourselves and others.

(Dag Hammarskjold)

Question: What machinery of forgiveness do you use? How often do you use it?

Prayer: Lord Jesus, from the Cross you taught us the art of forgiveness. People really don't know what they do by sinning. None of us does. Grace us with the skill to forgive as you have forgiven us.

7 Those Ordinary Virtues

St. Francis de Sales, a doctor of the Church, understood human psychology well. His advice is simple, direct, and clear. We are "little" people who need "little" virtues for the ordinary lives we live. Like that of another doctor of the Church, St. Thérèse of Lisieux, his way is not extraordinary or reserved for spiritual giants. Like the wisdom of St. Paul, we are to do the truth in love and use the ordinary virtues of humility and patience, tolerance and affability to achieve God's will for us.

> Let us go by land since the high sea is overwhelming and makes me seasick. Let us stay at our Lord's feet, like Mary Magdalene whose feast we are celebrating, and practice those ordinary virtues suited to our littleness — little peddler, little pack — these are the virtues which are better practiced in going downhill than in climbing, and suit our legs better: patience, forbearance toward our neighbor, service to others, humility, gentleness of heart, affability, tolerance of our own imperfections,

and similar little virtues. I do not say we are not to ascend by prayer, but that we do so one step at a time.

(Francis de Sales, Jane de Chantal)

Questions: Which ordinary virtue is God calling you to practice?

Prayer: Lord Jesus, may we sit at your feet in our littleness and long to be instructed in your ways. You know our needs better than we do. Send your Spirit that we may know and do what you ask of us.

Sources

P. 7: *Raissa's Journal*, presented by Jacques Maritain (Albany, NY: Magi Books, Inc., 1974), 71.

P. 10: Henri J. M. Nouwen, *The Genesee Diary: Report from a Trappist Monastery* (New York: Doubleday & Company, Inc. 1976), 59.

P. 12: Henry David Thoreau, *Walden and Civil Disobedience* (New York: Barnes & Noble Classics, 2003), 86-87.

P. 14: Loren Eiseley, *All the Strange Hours: The Excavation of a Life* (New York: Charles Scribner's Sons, 1975), 91.

P. 16: Richard J. Foster, *Freedom of Simplicity* (New York: Harper Paper-backs, 1981), p. 234.

P. 18: John Macquarrie, *In Search of Humanity: A Theological and Philosophical Approach* (New York: Crossroad, 1985), 146.

P. 20: James J. Bacik and Kevin E. Anderson, *A Light Unto My Path: Crafting Effective Homilies* (New York: Paulist Press, 2006), 56. With permission from Paulist Press.

P. 22: *Creative Prayer* by Brigid E. Herman edited by Hal M. Helms © 1999 by the Community of Jesus, used by permission Paraclete Press (www.paracletepress.com http://www.paracletepress.com), 14.

P. 26: *Francis de Sales, Jane de Chantal: Letters of Spiritual Direction*, trans. by Peronne Marie Thibert, V.H.M (New York: Paulist Press, 1988), 159. With permission from Paulist Press.

P. 28: Mohandas K. Gandhi, *AUTOBIOGRAPHY: The Story of My Experiments with Truth*, translated by Mahadev Desai (New York: Dover Publications, Inc., 1948), 394.

P. 30: Robert Morneau, *Gift, Mystery, and Calling: Prayers and Reflections* (Winona, MN: Saint Mary's Press, 1994), 52.

P. 32: Whittaker Chambers, *Witness* (New York: Random House, Inc., 1952), 109-110.

P. 34: William James, *The Varieties of Religious Experience: A Study of Human Nature* © 1952 by Whittaker Chambers. Used with permission of Random House, Inc. (New York: The Modern Library, 1936), 364.

P. 36: Nikos Kazantzakis, *Report to Greco*, translated by P. A. Bien (New York; Simon and Schuster, 1961), 487.

P. 38: *The HarperCollins Study Bible*: New Revised Standard Version (New York: HarperCollins Publishers, 1989), 2190.

P. 22: *Creative Prayer* by Brigid E. Herman edited by Hal M. Helms © 1999 by the Community of Jesus, used by permission Paraclete Press (www.paracletepress.com http://www.paracletepress.com), 14.

P. 44: Thomas Merton, *Seeds of Contemplation* (New York: Dell Publishing Co., Inc., 1949), 103.

P. 46: Gerald Vann, O. P., and P. K. Meagher, O. P., *The Devil and How to Resist Him* (Manchester, New Hampshire: Sophia Institute Press, 1957), 92.

P. 48: Parker Palmer, *Let Your Life Speak: Listening for the Voice of Vocation* (San Francisco: Jossey-Bass Inc. Publishers, 2000), 70.

P. 49: Thomas Keating, *Open Mind, Open Heart: A Contemplative Dimension of the Gospel* (New York: Continuum, 1986, 1997), 97.

P. 50: *The Selected Poetry of Jessica Powers*, edited by Regina Siegfried, ASC, and Robert F. Morneau (Washington, DC: ICS Publications, 1999), 92.

P. 52: Evelyn Underhill, *The Ways of the Spirit* (New York: Crossroad Publishing Co., 1993), 120.

P. 54: *The Spiritual Life: Selected Writings of Albert Schweitzer*, edited by Charles R. Joy (Hopewell, New Jersey: The Ecco Press, 1947), 98.

P. 58: Eugene A. Walsh, S.S., *Practical Suggestions for Celebrating Sunday Mass* (Glendale, AZ: Pastoral Arts Associates of North America, 1978), 30.

P. 60: Hannah Arendt, *The Human Condition* (Chicago: The University of Chicago Press, 1958), 243. With permission from the publisher.

P. 62: Hans Urs von Balthasar, *Prayer*, trans. by A. V. Littledale (New York: Sheed & Ward, 1961), 114.

P. 64: Ralph Waldo Emerson, *"Spiritual Laws," The Selected Writings of Ralph Waldo Emerson*, edited, with a biographical introduction by Brooks Atkinson (New York: Random House, 1940), 51.

P. 65: Ralph Waldo Emerson, *"Character,"* ibid., 165.

P. 66: Lawrence Elliott, *I Will Be Called John* (New York: Reader's Digest Press, E. P. Dutton & Co., Inc., 1973), 195.

P. 68: Walter Brueggemann, *The Prophetic Imagination* (Fortress Press, 1978), 83.

P. 69: Dag Hammarskjold, *Markings*, translated by Leif Sjoberg & W. H. Auden (New York: Alfred A. Knopf, 1981), 124.

P. 70: Francis de Sales, *Jane de Chantal: Letters of Spiritual Direction*, trans. by Peronne Marie Thibert, V.H.M (New York: Paulist Press, 1988), 98.